Forests of the Medieval World

Forests of the Medieval World

Don Coles

The Porcupine's Quill, Inc.

CANADIAN CATALOGUING IN PUBLICATION DATA

Coles, Don, 1928-
  Forests of the medieval world

Poems.
ISBN 0-88984-158-6

I. Title.

PS8555.O439F77   1993   C811'.54   C93-093754-6
PR9199.3.C76F77   1993

Published by The Porcupine's Quill, Inc., 68 Main
Street, Erin, Ontario NOB ITO with financial assistance
from The Canada Council and the Ontario Arts
Council. The support of the Government of Ontario
through the Ministry of Culture and Communications is
also gratefully acknowledged.

Trade orders to General Distribution Services,
34 Lesmill Road, Don Mills, Ontario M3B 2T6.

Readied for the press by John Metcalf.

Cover is after a photograph taken by Jennifer Dickson
at Villa Garzoni, Tuscany. All interior illustrations by
Virgil Burnett.

Second printing, November 1993.

I dreamt last night of my own
Death. As I died, I became the
Wren Library in Nevile's Court in
Trinity College, Cambridge. Dying,
The library became even more
Luminous, its splendid thinly leaded
Clerestory windows were lighting up
Even more valuably.

I tried to phone a cab
To go downtown but the line went
Dead!

My wife was moved. She had
A new friend already, however.

Sophie S., a friend of mine,
Though not that sort of friend,
Was even more moved. She found
A poem of mine describing all this
And rewrote it, in rhyming verse.
'Oh my little bicycle' was one of
Her lines. I knew I would not have
Published the poem in this form.

At a certain point I wept.
Up to this point I had kept my death
From everyone (although they knew).

When I wept the Wren Library
Did not tremble – I had feared
It would. Its clerestory luminosity,
Which was of course *my* clerestory
Luminosity, grew even more coolly
Elegant and uninhabited.

Its lack of inhabitants
Was what made its unearthly beauty
Glow so.

After my weeping, my wife and
Her new friend were more moved
Even than before.

           It was my heart,
The cause.

My son was in the general area.
In general, there was a feeling of
A certain amount of sorrow.

But I didn't want to worry
My son, who is fond of me,
And is eleven.

I was concerned about the taxi.
Would my beautiful windows oscillate
Too much on the trip downtown,
And shiver into thousands of
Tiny spears?

People were walking up and down
On the gravelled paths of
Trinity's Nevile's Court.

My death had been inevitable.

My son's face kept turning up,
Like a moon among all these things.

Driving in the car with her
Was wonderful! So close –
He loved, without any rush
To say so,

Those guileless uncoverings of
Legs getting in, their confidential
Jostlings as long as he kept
His foot down, the car

Moving in the tunnel of itself
Narrowing their options to
Crossing or uncrossing, or just
Dumbly offering themselves

Usually neatly together, which was
Fine, or now and then
Faintly apart. Amazing
How much good will

Their speechlessness built,
Also their apparent autonomy,
Not acknowledging her subtle face
Up above them even once,

While on the windshield
Loomed and fled
Whole transparencies of clouds and leaves
As he drove – unused pastorals

Stacking up behind. No matter
Whether, rearranging herself, she
Occasionally pointed them towards him
Or away, the car's
Little hurtling sky
Kept them close, and unmolested
Unless by a pensive hand,
Inadvertently. O Love,

The flawless creatures said,
Only we two can move your mind
To its ghost-marks, always,
And keep you from life's weariness.

Someone has stayed in Stockholm ever since
I left. He sold the motorbike (I used to
find it sheltered under plastic after rain,
I never knew who put that there and never tried
to find out, why not, I wonder? – ah, I was
rushing away from my image-free life,
is why) and eventually got a serious job,
he may even have married about when I did,
perhaps he married Caisa –
why not, why *wouldn't* he like
milky-skinned girls with red hair, was he
crazy or something? Now his Swedish is
perfect, his kids have both had their
stipendium-years in Paris, and he spends
summers on the west coast, at Tylösand,
near Bostad, they like it for its beach and
the big-time tennis every July. If he regrets
anything it's having failed to show up
back home for those two major deaths,
nothing to do with staving them off but
there's always that gap because
you didn't speak a remedying sentence
in time, right? And by now you've guessed
what it was. I could expand but I won't. Back
to him, some lunchtimes he walks along Strandvägen,
its elegant melancholy facades, he admires
the boats tied up there, if the sun's out there's
those tiny blindings off the water, and if
he wants to he can head for the Old Town and take
interesting ways back. But what else
has he done? Has he lain on his bed and

realized he has this whole unobserved life
to idle in? To turn his car
in directions I didn't, and bring
all those roads into the headlights?
What roads? That's the point! Fine, but
there are other things than motion,
you know. Yes but whatever his headlights
touch is a bonus, even that late-night fence-post
whitening and then lost again
shouldn't be underrated, every image makes
a special offer when it knows
you decided against it the first time. He
could simply be remembering an old half-hour
when he was bored in the schoolroom and
had a mysterious unfinished thought about
how his life will turn out — there's
nothing remarkable about this except that perhaps
he remembers it often whereas I'm only
remembering it now and only because of
him, because of the extra time he has. Or
he could be standing on the escalator and there's
a woman going the opposite way who
looks at him so intensely for
as long as it takes her to ride past
that he longs for her all day, or even
switches directions and catches up to her,
but what happens then? Who knows. Maybe
she says Oh that was just the look
I give men whose devotion I want for only
a few seconds, time's up, on the other hand
she could have recognized him from

some other life or escalator. But
this is what I mean. Whatever he does
is innocent because he never waves or
makes a sudden move, and this is
something I think about a lot and which
words cannot soothe. Although you can
fall into places deeper than language,
can't you? Yes. He has.

My Son at the Seashore, Age Two

He laughs and a breeze
lifts his hair. His face tilts up
towards what has happened
to his hair, that it should lift,
and his laugh goes. Why
is this happening, his suddenly
serious face wants to know, and
what is happening. But
all it is is a little breeze
lifting his hair for a few seconds,
a little breeze passing by
on its way to oblivion –
as this day is on its way there too,
and as that day, twenty years ago,
was, too.

Night Game

Supper over, and with not much time left before we
Decamp from this weekend with my Dad,
I wander out towards the park for air.
He's already back into his duel to the
Death, I mean it, with the TV, where
Teams x and y are manoeuvring on some
Nebulous, perpetual ground. There's
A game on out here too, I see –
Industrial League softball, scoreboard claims it's
Triple Star Cleaners vs. Harper's Electric.
Shortsleeve shirts confirm. Hardly dusk
But they're already under the lights.
'Way to look, Gary, way to look!' seems to, yes, *does*
Come from the third-base coach, though long before
The exclamation-mark he's browsing among
The interior stitchings of his stripey green cap:
He's hung around one base or another out here
A few hundred times before, that one,
I think the message is. Two on –
I'll just see if they bring them in. Although
Two down, too. Oh well, hmm. Funny banter,
Back-and-forth ribbings among the bluejeaned families,
And players from an earlier or still-upcoming game
Spotted here and there. Usual comings and goings,
Nods, little signals. It's a soft night. Sitting
Where I am right now I'm farther away, it
Occurs to me, from my agreed-upon present life
Than I've been for a long while. And now Gary pops up,
Stranding both of them, and mindlessly cast down
At this development I'm beginning to plot
My smartest route sideways and down among the families

When here on his way past our end of the bleacher
And now right in front of us, momentarily pausing
For an exchange of quips with the arriving Star
Third-baseman, comes the greencapped coach, and
I know his name, I know the street he lived on
Thirty years ago, and I know exactly how old he is
Right now. Who once of his own accord
Opted out of a richly promising – from *his*
Point of view, though never mine – schoolyard free-for-all
To sit on that school's cement steps with me when
I'd stopped a punch to what we used to call the solar plexus
That left me winded and incapable and ashamed.
We sat until my breath remembered its way back,
Saying only occasional things, and then walked off
Together to somewhere below memory. His act,
Relinquishing that stage he was so good on, astonished
Me then, though I never told him so,
And does so still, seeing him here – he might
With equal probability, that day, have mentioned
Kierkegaard, or Brahms. And now has ambled back
To his bench and is sitting there, his green cap
Tugged straight-visored onto his greyish crewcut head,
Staring into the evening diamond. Lornie Hart, who
One day with no warning stepped out of the corridor
That led to all my proliferating classrooms,
Closing off a decade shared as never another would be,
And set off towards tonight by a clandestine route.
Does he still work at that plant, by now
Service Manager, Parts Division, did he marry
One of those girls we leaned on our handlebars
To watch, oh, wherever we happened to come

Across them? No, skip that, the condescension and
All of it: say this instead — he has just dropped in from some
Intricate adventure to rest here, replenish
His special energies before slipping away
As the whole town knows he must, knows
He always has and always will, gone from the corridor,
Its quick capricious son. I watch him here, I'm
Testing plans of approach, but none of my scenarios
Seems promising: our words will surely stall
In a formal distance we never knew or learned
To deal with. Shown these thoughts of mine
Lornie will think *No, this isn't how it is.*
This is not how either of us used to think.
And the game proceeds. Ten minutes and I'll
Have to be back on the road to the city.
Lornie Hart hunches forward on his bench,
Guarding something of me. Those two boys who
Hugged their knees in the sunlight, talking sparingly
Of anything that was not a punch, waiting
For enough indifference to gather in them
To allow them to get up and go, they are more
His property than mine, they are more at home here
Than anywhere I can get to. They'll fade again
From me, they'll be a little further off
During my walk back to the house even, but
Down there on the bench their brief voices
Are vibrant and near.

I Walk by this Shore

I walk by this shore
while the waves roll
out of the dark. In

the last half-hour the lake
has gone imageless, or almost,
out there now only

white phosphorings randomly
prick the dark. How often with
this same incuriosity

I've observed these
remote and opaque signals –
such pointless

claims for attention! – but
just now it's their familiarity
that seems to be loosening

the easy downwards slope
towards being young, and
taking advantage of

whatever's there I ask, 'Will you
follow me as far back as I want
to go?' (shouldn't have,

right away there's an imminent
paling but) the dream's dark persists
and asserts strong hold –

here on the shore
the surprised years now
start up. Voices and

the resumed cries of children
impinge, their discrete calls mirror
the hidden extensions

of the lake; the sky turns
milky-white and everyone
is again just as they

wanted to be, each face shows
something beyond what it will
ever reach. This must be

innocence, the little waves
on their remembered way past
release mornings full of

more feelings than you could ever
use up during the day, also
expanses of playing

that were always there and lasted
on and on — and I stand
in the shadowless water

which made us all one
while our vast adventures waited
to form. Strange how

those adventures, which we were sure
were waiting for us, really
happened! We have all become

something! But now as
the becoming-something starts, the children
are looking irresolute. The sky

is darkening or growing pale
and they're standing looking outwards
at the darkening or paling

sky, while on the lake
those small sporadic crestings
of white still ignite

and roll minutely. And now they're
gone, not the whitecaps but
the children, yes,

it must have been time
to go in, the shore and
the lake too

so dark now, it must have
been as far as any of us
wanted to come.

'Today I saw my daughter, Mitzi, my favourite,
with her baby, smiling and smiling', she was tellin' us this
   mornin'.
She never had no daughter, pore old thing.

'This is not Paradise, I don't care
what you say', that one over there's been cryin' out,
'It is insipid from dawn till dusk!'

This one here now, many's the time
I've heard her greet visitors askin'
with her teeth clackin' away,
'How're the Free French?'
She really is a caution.

Sure, mostly women here, they live longer....

      — In room after room
long-dead fathers counsel their troubled daughters,
                     accidentally grown old,
with yearned-after, secret, caressing voices.

I awoke with a feeling of clarity, a feeling diaphanous as a lake at dawn, as clichéd as that but undismissable, the lake itself then spreading out before me. The sudden patience of it among that congestion of trees and low bushes – you knew your life should always have been like this.

From the opposite shore came sounds of several brief unapprehended lives.

The ten fingers of someone's two hands were pressing into my back like little warm pools.

Parts of many ideas were beginning to be visible to me.

I had not sustained any damage at all yet. Whatever was special in me had not been dulled by use or exposure or by being thought about. This was the main thing.

Nothing used to be better than it was now.

A vagueness on the shore of the lake was revealed as the sum of all happiness. Within a minute or two I knew this couldn't be true. But most happiness.

I was waiting for the images to start. There were no books, nobody had ever died, the first wave would soon think itself in from the lake.

He taps the adjectives and verbs of love
Onto his screen. They infiltrate
The green and faintly glowing ground,
Arriving not from below
Or either side or above
But as if they've been sown here long ago,
These tiny, darkfaced seeds of self, and made to wait
During quite a few years of
Not exactly being alone, but worse. So straight
And tidy they are, plus the small pure sound
When they tip up out of the green,
He thinks they're bound
To be better than what's normally around,
Aren't they? Meanwhile behind the verdurous screen
Something's impending. What can it be?
Far off, never to be seen
Hereabouts, but the cause of everything? It's she.

(G.A.Henty, author of some dozens of turn-of-the-century
books for boys; titles were and are *With Clive in India, With
Wolfe in Canada, True to the Old Flag,* et al.)

All these hefty pinkboarded volumes
on the secondhand shelves inscribed in
faded blue fountain-pen, 'To James,
on his 12th, with congratulations
from us both, Michaelmas term 1902',
or *circa* – messages, they seem now, about
how easy it was to grow up once,
and although we'll worry later about
the brownskinned and salaaming nameless ones, meanwhile
we browse and prickle pleasurably.

'A lad stood on a little lookout
turret', or, 'Shading their eyes against
the sun shining low across the Irrawaddy'
– so they began, and faithfully
begin still, Henty's young men
gazing at *something* (always a high-percentage
thing to do: the stared-at jungle will
bulge, from faraway out of the desert's
heat-haze the Mahdi's silken pennants
will tinily ripple), standing shoulder
to shoulder at the railing of the P. & O. liner
on its way to Calcutta, to the Transvaal, to
the Plains of Abraham, lifting and lowering
a little on those tons of blue water
en route towards wherever the Empire
requires them –

          – 'towards themselves',
more recent decades would propose, but
not this turn-of-the-century one. Here
the 'self' is still uninvented, almost
traitorous, probably ill-bred, and
nobody has brought a single *arrière-pensée*
with him. How safe it all feels! This
must be mostly because these young men
(subalterns and aides-de-camp and
the squirearchy's disinherited sons)
were when I first read of them
older than I was, as they were also older
than my father and my uncles when *they*
admired them first – so I didn't fret
that I hadn't done yet what they in
these thousands of pages were shown doing.
I was entitled to watch them still from
my room, from my moored childhood,
I could loiter aimlessly there
a while longer. And that they brought
so little, so nearly nothing with them
into these stories was reassuring. They
were as empty as I knew myself to be,
like me they faced a world full of images
which would surely fill them up, would surely
fill me up too – images from
the hill-stations of Simla or the laagered
wagons of the *voortrekkers* or who can divine
what else, nobody can, it's beyond us –
images, anyhow, from all over, baubles
and beguilements, the inexhaustible
icon-storehouse of the imperium.

And how sporting of them
to know nothing, apparently, about women!
If they knew more than the rumours that were
all I knew, they were honorable enough
to keep it to themselves. All that was
understood among us was that sometime,
safely homecome, a terrific girl
would appear – one for each of us,
out of her unvexed shire, summoned
by love. But not soon, not for
a long while: for years still she would have to
drowse in the future's heat-shimmer.
When she would finally appear, of course
we'd recognize her – all this gazing-practice
would stand us in good stead then. And
by then much else would be in plain view
as well. Everything that had been
mysterious off there below the horizons
of our voyages would be straightforward and
clear when they were over. Sated with
novelty we'd sail home to the waiting ones,
that quayside frieze of shyly-prouds who,
pausing only to assure us nothing had changed,
would fade away like the late-afternoon
sunlight across the lawns and tennis courts
and broad meadows of our inheritances.
Within a dozen pages, paragraphs even,
they'd be gone, it'd be our turn to be them,
manfully we'd get on with it.

        I lift the book and read,
and the words reach me like the voice, no,

not of family but of a long-unheard
neighbour, unmissed until now but likeable,
undemanding, familiar. How welcome,
how apparently valuable the words are,
sudden and calming as a wide bend in a river.
Aged ten and eleven I read shelf after shelf
of these things, nothing else so exactly right,
before putting them down forever. Forever
until now. Their sanguine, lulling rhythms
(oh, world-girdling smugnesses, appalling
certainties) have pulsed on on shelves like these
without a sound reaching me from them
all this while. From wherever I may be said
to be now, a kind of lookout perhaps,
shading my eyes perhaps, I gaze
back at them. In the outward world
hardly a shred of what they offered seems to be
left. No loss, of course, but it's not their
tiny heroics, rejected antics that are
coming clear now anyway, no, they're gesturing
in a direction I might never have looked
without them, never today anyhow, and quickly
and with what amazing ease now I'm entering
a place usually more darkly garrisoned by far
than any of those redoubts and drawbridged citadels
so common to all of them. It's inside, of course,
this room of the immortal images,
which even before I can guess who they are
stir, and wake, and now, pouring scenes
deeper than anything Henty's pages have access to,
pouring earliness, bear me home.

❧ Aporoi

I The Scythians, said the Greeks,
were always somewhere else—
they were *'aporoi'*. Unlike
the Scythians or us, the Greeks
preferred to be here.

II Others who are *aporoi*:
Amelia Earhart,
the All-Nite Speedy Plumbers,
Christ Risen. And one or two women
mentioned by friends of mine
in late-night conversations.

III Final *aporoi*: Christine Roux,
the original of Puccini's Musette,
who disappeared in 1860
after boarding a Rhône steamship
with 40,000 francs 'amassed
by prostitution'.

IV Photos of Christine naked
were all the police had to assist
their investigation. As if she was
getting ready to become a naiad
forever.

▒ Basketball Player and Friends

for my father, Jack Coles (1897-1986).
He was once the first-string right forward
of the University of Toronto Blues.

Here is a young man sitting
with his teammates for a college year-book photo,
bony-shouldered in his crested singlet and
plain white shorts on a front-row bench,
and looking, even though it's seventy years
since he and all these were substituted
for the last time, pretty much at home.
This may be because he has never entirely assented to
being done with all this, this bench, these
three rows of young men staring out
just as he is staring out, as opaquely;
and it may be only because the things
he and these young men know, things
so unequivocal in sunlight once, now
hidden in dateless night

> – long trajectory of the first throw
>   into the empty
>   gym, thudding vibrations of
>   ball off rim –
> – morning the bus broke down
>   outside Kingston, horsing around
>   in the zero morning, that frosh guard's
>   incredible limericks –
> – perfectly-understood slight
>   tilt of a head, feint of a body
>   trotting up the floor –

are by their own admission so irrelevant to
what's coming, incommunicable in any way that
the still-unmet intimate faces of their long lives
will ever, listening, really alter to,
that what we have here is one of those billions of
caves below words
people live in all over the place (fine by me
of course, better than most of the language-caves
I walk around in), but like many of them
kind of sad. Well, sad because of
its so-early relinquishing back there,
and its later-on tightlipped *Verbot* against
any honourable link with who they became...
but no, if I think about it, not *just* sad
when you remember what it does *not* show.
It does *not* show this young man
getting up from this bench to marry,
to assume the quasi-innocent khaki of 1916,
to make it home again and drive thereafter
through smalltown decades, year after year
the same five blocks, to the same office,
or, now that all that and much more than
all that is done with, to end up
watching TV, making foolish and repetitive errors
in conversation, sometimes guessing wrong
on a staircase, sleeping in stained bedclothes, and
what still pisses me off the most are
the letters he'd get from rarely-visiting
relatives who happened to be in need of
cash telling him how they loved him
best. The photo does not show

any of this. No, it shows him still here
with his teammates, all of them on
the frail bark bounding forward
on the dark wave, and all watching out
into the high-lifting dark, how life will be, patiently
with their camera-concentrated,
guileless, unprophetic eyes.

Forests of the medieval world, that's
where her mind will wander
the three dissertation years, lucky girl – ⸝
Forest of Bleu, which crowded around
the walls of Paris and stretched 10,000 leagues
in every direction; the great Hercynian forests
of East Prussia, from which each year
334 drovers bore the logs for the fires
in the Grand Duke's castles of Rostock,
of Danzig and, furthest east of all, guarding
the borders towards the Polish marshes,
Greifswald and Wolgast. I'm so sad
I could die, you said as you left, but
my children, how could I bear it –
and I know, I know there are ways
of losing children, of seeing them stray off
among the trees even now, especially now!
Every fleet needed for its construction
the razing of an entire forest –
lost forests meeting on the tilting hills
of the Caspian, the Baltic, the Black Sea,
over the mountains of water the file of forests
comes. Your face is a mobile mischief,
do you know? Your eyes mocked before
they entreated, your lips rendered
both comedy and its dark twin
in microseconds, and your tongue
harried my mouth's bays and inlets.

The *Oberforstmeister* of Kurland promised
the King 'at least half-fabulous' beasts
for the hunt, his forest measured
140,000 *arpents* and even on the swiftest mounts
horsemen could not traverse it
in a month. My mind runs fast
down its *arpents* and leafy corridors,
seeing no one, I should slash
tree-trunks to procure my safe return
but I can't stop. My mind is running
on pure grief and pure love, I want you
to know this. The Forest of Othe
was so still you could hear a shadow
cross a face at 60 leagues distance –
it had linked the Lyons Massif with
the Woods of Gisors but after a hurricane
levelled a million trees in 1519 the diligent
peasants moved in with plows and those forests
were never reunited. And
the forests of Finland, have you thought of those?
All the way to Archangel and the White Sea?
They can show you how you were
before these excuses. What can you do
about this, your exigent look said
in the doorway, I am going do you realize
I am going? And that both of us will survive this?
When the Swedes needed cash they cut down
the forests of Pomerania, the result in
many cases is sand-dunes. This for day-trippers
is nice, in your rented *Strandkorb* there is room
for everybody, also for dressing and undressing

when the beach is crowded. In the forest of Morois
Tristan lies with Iseult, they are waiting
for the King her husband who will tell history
they were only sleeping. In
the Black Forest dwarf trees and greenheart
still flourish — as for the Rominter Heide
it was so huge that most of its lakes
and forests were 'held in reserve',
not listed or even mentioned, so for generations
all that those lakes and forests could do was
grow uncontrollably in the imagination. I
would take you with me into the Rominter Heide
if you would come: there
each child we must not hurt will
wear a rose in sign of her ardent, forbearing
heart, in sign of his calm-eyed ascent through
our extreme, necessary years.

*The poems are based on a number of
paintings by the Norwegian artist
Edvard Munch, and on his (largely-
untranslated) diaries. My thanks
to the Director of the Munch Museum
in Oslo, Arne Eggum, for permission to
browse among those diaries, and to my
much-younger self for stopping off
for a few years in Scandinavia, long
enough to learn to read those several
languages. Most of the poems share
titles with the paintings they take
their points of departure from; it
will be understood that some are
offered in the voice of E.M., some
not. I'll add only that E.M.
returned obsessively throughout
his long working life to a very few
themes from childhood or early manhood —
these include the death of his mother
when he was four, the death of his
sister Sophie, his love for 'Fru H.',
his loneliness.*

to Edvard Munch

'det ubevidste Sjaeleliv' †

† *the unknown life of the soul*

When she was dying Mama asked us to
be good and love Jesus
so she could travel up to the angels
with an easy mind.
Vil Du lovar mig det?
Ja. †
But in Berlin each little door
opened to a waiting white body
and the woman said, 'Perhaps
you'd prefer a chubby one?', and
'Yes', I said. Almost everything
should be simpler than it is.

† *Will you promise me that?*
  Yes.

▒ Sick Child

for Johanne Sophie Munch,
b. 1862, d. of tuberculosis 1877.
Edvard barely survived the same
disease a year later.

After Mother, I loved you
best. Daddy and me
tried to keep you but
God wouldn't answer. How
it cooked in your breast!
You haemorrhaged all the images
you meant to grow towards.
When I got to your age I almost
burst – the hand-towels crimsoned
all day long.
> *Jesus help me*
> *I'm dying, do you think*
> *I'll go to Heaven if I die?*
> *I think you will, min kaere son.*
If I'd have been older, I'd have
saved you. As for the 'thousand
Sophies', all those versions,
what they've written about those
is *mad*. The reason I kept on
sketching you's got nothing to do with
keeping you close, affirming you, guilt,
whatever else they've guessed –
I was only trying to outnumber Death.

Brothers are *difficult*. Consider
the James boys (I mean
the brainy ones, not those
moronic bandits), super to everyone
except each other – H. fled even adored Venice
when W. got too near. As for
die Gebrüder Mann†, same story:
when a reviewer slates Heinrich
for being (on his first try, this was)
'no playwright', Thomas's diary
notes briskly, 'True. And Heini's
no novelist, either'. *Schlimm, sowas.* ‡
But here now in a painting by
his brother Edvard is
Peter Andreas Munch,
seated before a bookcase,
reading. Twelve years later, aged 30
and only a few months married
he will write to his family
'I can't stand life anymore', and
die. Nobody will find out why,
though the family never liked
his wife. It is necessary
to know this as you watch him
read. He is eighteen years old
and what he is doing here seems
simple, seems quiet, seems
preferable to much else he could be up to.

† *the brothers Mann*
‡ *tough, that sort of thing*

I believe one or two world-religions are
palimpsested beneath that preference.
Or here he is again, exiting
from the bedroom in which Sophie,
eternally fifteen and pillowed
in her wicker chair is, as usual,
dying. Typically, no fuss:
Peter Andreas has chosen for his exit
a moment when nobody's looking.
The rest of them (Inger, Laura, Edvard
inside his own canvas, and over there
Papa and Aunt Karen) are all present
but engaged, heads bowed,
hands clasped, this is
grief's familiar iconography. They are
vulgar by comparison. Not to compete
with them, to eschew as he does
this *tableau* hardly at all *vivant*,
to efface himself so, is surely
a class act. He leaves observed by
no one alive in the world then
and enters a quiet which even his brother,
facing away in this scene (and painting it
only years later) will forever deny
he heard. You,
seeing this now, in that Oslo gallery or
as this page turns, endure
the private arrow. The arrow
privately.

This is enough,
almost. Just one glimpse more.
Peter Andreas's childhood drawings,
preserved who knows why, show scores of
single file Red Indians, matchstick-men
in feathered headdresses, queueing across
page after page of a schoolboy's scribbler
to attack a stockaded fort,
their conciliatory gait and slack tomahawks
in no hurry even though
the cannonballs, black and neat and
trailing terrific threads of wind,
are unmistakably *en route* towards them.
This is, the gallery's pamphlet says,
'Arithmetical art ... without value',
but I recognize
my own unpraised childish imaginings,
an identical tribe wandering there,
and feel Peter Andreas near. It reminds me
of my chance to be like him,
to go back to where I could see myself
as I might have been
before things showed themselves to me,
and then say
this has not happened,
or this, or this. Back to where
I could heal all the air
I ever spoke through, and have
nobody thinking about me, ever.

        ...Who would
wish for that? No one. But
all the same. To sit
reading before the bookcase,
the one you have almost forgotten,
a long time ago,
at home. To draw Red Indians.
To leave that room without saying much.

🕮 *Death of Marat*

We travelled south, to Dresden,
drinking all day and then making
love, which weakened me still
more —
                    E.M.'s diary

Charlotte Corday stands naked
beside a murdered man on a bed.

'Look what I've done!'

Quarts of blood but no knife.

If this is a puzzle, it is
easily solved. She has killed him
with her nakedness. Now
breasts, belly, all those
good parts and
the perfunctorily painted face
have rotated towards us. We
understand it is our turn and
face up to this like men.

Ibsen stood beside me
a long while looking.
He seemed more interested
in the spermflowing margins
than in Death thrusting his
spindleshank between her thighs,
or her ripe belly pressing
against and apparently massaging
an everlasting absence – or
something very hard
to guess the nature of. It
reminded me how Fru H.'s†
soft body would give
way, and give way, and how
her mouth would go down, and
down, and I said
the world is always useless
without just this one human being,
isn't it. Ibsen replied
he found it painful to
look at young girls, though
he'd be helped from now on
remembering their smooth bodies
were not durable. He then said
his own body had been
silent for years.

† *Fru H. – She is usually so identified in Munch's diaries,*
   and although biographers have since told us her name,
   we can leave it as Munch left it. She was a married
   woman and the very young E.M. had a brief affair with her.
   He was probably in love with her for the rest of his life.

Summer Evening by the Lake

I am painting her standing among
the white birches and watching
the moonlight's broad track across the water.

Even from the back there is
a definite resemblance to
the unknown woman I long for.

This is partly because of what she is doing.

Naturally I have wondered about
her face. I have gestured in the vicinity with
my loaded-up brush.

But I was afraid it would be in tears.

No, he never saw her so, his wife naked
under her dress in trifling talk
with somebody in that dark garden
down there — but he thought it.
If he could trade this in for
a sadder thought he would.
Now any pause by day or night
lights it up inside, her body's gentle
tips and declivities
unshadow the world, he can't believe
such blatant bliss escapes anybody.
There must be another day somewhere,
the *real* day of which the day when
this thought first occurred to him
is the false copy, he tells himself —
when not only didn't this happen
but the guess at its possibility
is forbidden. Now all his exciting plans
for love seem gone with her white body
into a disordered and dark garden,
he feels his life rushing towards
being alone, and as for the son
they used to say they were going to have,
he won't be able to carry him
on his shoulders, now, ever,
as he wanted to, will he.

And here is one who is only a little part of the idea
she will become. You would like as you see her
on her enormous bed to find words that will assist her
towards the idea she will become, or save her from it
if this is what you would rather, but your words
will have to be very good, the idea may be as unmanageable
as seeing her here is to you. Your words may have to be
as good as Prince Andrey's were for Pierre Bézuhov
on that dusty road near the Prince's summer estate of
Bogutcharovo when the two men rode together all the
     afternoon
of August 26, 1809, Pierre noticing the heat and dust
on the leaves of the birch trees while they rode
and remembering long afterwards how certain important
     words
first reached his mind only inches
above the darkbrown, sweating and glistening motion of the
     horse
which seemed to carry him easily forward among the
     important words,
so easily he knew he might never forget them –
although probably she is too incomplete, this one,
to receive words like those, you cannot expect *her*
to nod and reflect and ride on slowly beside you
knowing she is in a specially resonating seashell
of language that will never be bettered and that will
change her life.

As for me
while I stood before her in the Munchmusé in Oslo
feeling her incompleteness beginning to flow towards me,
a woman passing nearby paused and seemed
to fall into some thought of her own for a few minutes.
I think she was 30, of average height and build, blonde hair
in a short, straight cut, wearing grey slacks and
a red cashmere cardigan over a white small-collared shirt,
and her face was the most beautiful I have ever seen.
Not to have seen it would have changed nothing
I have done since, although some thoughts. Where the stasis
or on the other hand the outflowings
of art come in here is that there is nothing
in stone or bronze or on all the holy ceilings of Christendom
that will outlast that face among the images of my life,
even though I have totally forgotten it now. I mention her
     here
because I have no other way, since her thought's pause
ended and she walked far off from me, to alter her
     relationship
to decay or to death.

What they didn't like took me years
to understand. What they *said* it was
was the serving-maid on the rumpled
conjugal bed or a madonna's
equivocal sweating or even
Hans Jaeger's† coffeehouse rhetoric,
as if I needed smoky talk to decide
where the paint went. But these weren't
what they really hated. It wasn't even
those solitary ones I showed
gazing across a salt-stirring sea
towards something perfect they once saw —
those horizon-aching women who were
almost 40 now and so unused,
so quietly, quietly unused. Women
saw them and kept just as quiet
as who they were seeing;
men imagined, finding them new,
they could save them.
　　　　　　　No, what they really
couldn't abide, or if they could
couldn't stand their wives'
learning about, was *nothing. Nothing*
was what they didn't like. What
frightened them. That madonna, who
could have been lying back anywhere, being
worshipped or fucked, or Sophie dying
in her chair by the window
with its flowerpot, and then dying

† *Hans Jaeger was the leader of a so-called Bohemian*
　set in Oslo frequented by the young E.M.

minus all of those, *no* chair *no*
window *no* flowerpot, nothing but
loose brown colour around both those lives,
all the detail gone, the skirtingboards, pupils
in the eyes, all of it rubbed away,
smeared over, dug out with the brush's
butt-end, even the floorboards
unreliable — *that's* what was
upsetting, the framelessness of
everything. All those things which
people feel confused by
which you'd better not deprive them of.
If the rims of our lives go imageless
anything at all can drift in there,
a long glance for instance —
how do you cope with that? Or
you might think you want to give yourself
completely to somebody, and if
there's no surroundings
it could all at once be hard not to —
all your trees, piano lessons, holidays, little looks
you've been on the receiving end of
ever since you started, they'd all go
with you and there'd be nothing left
anywhere to just wait for you, to show
a way back from this somebody
if you needed it sometime. Of course
it's frightening! And yet we all guess
it's the only place to really
find ourselves in, don't we?
A place with no furniture? No books,
no people, no plants on the window-ledge?

All those things we never really wanted
that are always there? Oh,
we've always known this – that
anything complicated is a lie. So
coming now in sight of it, the lies
pouring out of the sides of the canvases,
must have felt contagious and worrying,
especially to people who would be bound
to realize that others seeing this
could understand it too. Others
who lived with them and wished every day
they didn't. All of them together now
falling into a place where no word
had ever been. Like Sophie, sickening
all those months in the same room,
her eyes taking back all the images
the room had ever had, taking them back inside
just by looking at them so many hours. Finally
without anything at all to look at or be safe in.
You're not supposed to admit
that this happens – especially
if you do what I do, if you make things.
But it does, you know.

A skinny old party in a too-big suit
has just turned the lights on
at a quarter past three. What
does he do now? Where is everybody?
He is just realizing nobody has told him
how to be as old as this. Another way
of putting it: nobody has taught old age
how to enter him. He's wondering
why has he painted himself into this room
which so obviously has got only
a few minutes left in it. Just inches
below the paint's surface in that canvas
over there the shadowy damp breasts
of that woman remind him of something.
Was it worth her while, once, to love him?
He remembers a night-fulcrum —
those breasts swaying close over his eyes
again and again, half the night it seems,
coming over like moons, his mouth too
was continuously amazed. He always knew
descriptions of happiness must remain illegible
but you can stay close to it if you don't move,
can't you? No you can't. These did, though —
glistening from his own young mouth, too;
an hour's immortal even if a life isn't.

Contents

The Edvard Munch Poems

'My Death as the Wren Library', 'Driving in the Car with Her', 'Jealousy', and 'Forests of the Medieval World' were published in *The London Review of Books;* 'Night Game' in *The Malahat Review;* 'Basketball Player and Friends' in *Ariel;* 'Lapidary Voices from the Nursing Home' and 'Princesse Lointaine' in *Soho Square III;* 'Someone has Stayed in Stockholm' in *The North;* some of the 'Edvard Munch Poems' in the *The Second Macmillan Anthology;* and 'Remembering Henty' and 'I Walk by this Shore' in *The Third Macmillan Anthology.*

Don Coles was born in Woodstock, Ontario. He studied at Cambridge University and lived in Europe for a number of years, returning to Canada in the 60s. Coles' books of poetry include *The Prinzhorn Collection*, *Landslides: Selected Poems 1975-1985*, *K. in Love* and *Little Bird*. Don Coles teaches at York University in the Division of Humanities and lives in Toronto.